STRATEGY GAMES

By
Kirsty Holmes

CRABTREE
PUBLISHING COMPANY
WWW.CRABTREEBOOKS.COM

CRABTREE
PUBLISHING COMPANY
WWW.CRABTREEBOOKS.COM

Published in Canada
Crabtree Publishing
616 Welland Avenue
St. Catharines, ON
L2M 5V6

Published in the United States
Crabtree Publishing
PMB 59051
350 Fifth Ave, 59th Floor
New York, NY 10118

Published in 2019 by Crabtree Publishing Company

Author: Kirsty Holmes

Editors: Holly Duhig, Petrice Custance

Design: Gareth Liddington

Proofreader: Melissa Boyce

**Production coordinator and
prepress technician:** Margaret Amy Salter

Print coordinator: Katherine Berti

All facts, statistics, web addresses and URLs in this book were verified as valid and accurate at time of writing. No responsibility for any changes to external websites or references can be accepted by either the author or publisher.

Printed in the U.S.A./012019/CG20181123

Photo credits:
All images are courtesy of Shutterstock.com.

Cover – , 2 - Swill Klitch, 4 - Swill Klitch, 5 - Giuseppe_R, Saikorn, Niphon Subsri, 10 - Blan-k, A-spring, Prostock-studio, adamziaja.com, 11 - GooGag, IconBunny, 18 - VitalityVill, 22 - pluie_r, 23 - Evan-Amos, Boffy b, Images are courtesy of Shutterstock.com. With thanks to Getty Images, Thinkstock Photo and iStockphoto.

Civilization VI: Images courtesy of 2K Games, Inc. and Take-Two Interactive Software, Inc. All rights reserved. The Great Falls Gamers: Images courtesy of Jeff Nation and JJ Locke, with grateful thanks to all the Great Falls Gamers. StarCraft: all images courtesy of Blizzard Entertainment, Inc. Worm: all images courtesy of Team17, all rights reserved. With grateful thanks.

Library and Archives Canada Cataloguing in Publication

Holmes, Kirsty, author
        Strategy games / Kirsty Holmes.

(Game on!)
Includes index.
Issued in print and electronic formats.
ISBN 978-0-7787-5269-1 (hardcover).--
ISBN 978-0-7787-5330-8 (softcover).--
ISBN 978-1-4271-2191-2 (HTML)

1. Electronic games--Juvenile literature. 2. War games--Juvenile literature. 3. Fantasy games--Juvenile literature. I. Title.

GV1469.15.H648 2018   j794.8   C2018-906135-9
                                                                            C2018-906136-7

Library of Congress Cataloging-in-Publication Data

Names: Holmes, Kirsty, author.
Title: Strategy games / Kirsty Holmes.
Description: New York, New York : Crabtree Publishing Company, 2019. |
   Series: Game On! | Includes index. | Audience: Age 9-12. | Audience:
   Grade 4 to 6.
Identifiers: LCCN 2018053429 (print) | LCCN 2018055652 (ebook) |
   ISBN 9781427121912 (Electronic) |
   ISBN 9780778752691 (hardcover : alk. paper) |
   ISBN 9780778753308 (pbk. : alk. paper)
Subjects: LCSH: Video games--Juvenile literature. | Strategy--Juvenile
   literature.
Classification: LCC GV1469.3 (ebook) | LCC GV1469.3 .H68 2019 (print) |
   DDC 794.8--dc23
LC record available at https://lccn.loc.gov/2018053429

CONTENTS

WELCOME TO THE ARCADE

In what other games can you play as a Viking warrior, an Egyptian queen, or a starship commander? If you've picked up this book, you may have played **strategy** games before—maybe you've even won a few battles. This gaming guide will help you build your skills, taking you from the farm to the throne in the world of strategy games. So what are you waiting for? Let's get your game on!

Hey, gamer! I'm in the mood for a strategy game, but I can't decide who I want to play as. On the one hand, I could be Julius Caesar, leader of Rome. On the other hand, I could be Queen Elizabeth I of England and send my army of ships across the sea to Spain. Both sound fun. Who do you want to play as today?

Let's start at the beginning. A video game is an **electronic** game that needs a player (that's you!) to use a device to make stuff happen on a screen. Usually, that screen is a television or a personal computer (PC), but you can play games on smartphones, handheld gaming devices, and tablets. To play on your television you will need a **console**. There are lots of types of video games. From platformers and speed racers to amazing action-adventure games, there is an exciting amount of choice in the world of gaming!

Did you make a choice, gamer?
Let's step inside the Arcade...

<<Player One... Ready...?>>

ARCADE

DATA FILE: STRATEGY GAMES

Strategy games are games where thinking ahead is really important. Sometimes you have to develop a whole world from scratch, often starting with no supplies. You must gather **resources** and attempt to win the game by completing certain **objectives**. You may have to defeat all your neighbors or take over an area. In other games, you might be put in the middle of a situation, such as a war, and you must make your way through it. These games can be played with friends, either in the same room or online, or by yourself against the computer. Games vary in difficulty and how complicated they are. Most strategy games are played on a PC, but there are many available on smartphones as apps. They can also be played on consoles, but they can be difficult to control with a handheld controller. Most people prefer to play with a mouse and keyboard on a computer.

Arcade, we're ready to start. Load data.

<<LOADING... DATA LEVEL ONE: WHAT IS A STRATEGY GAME?>>

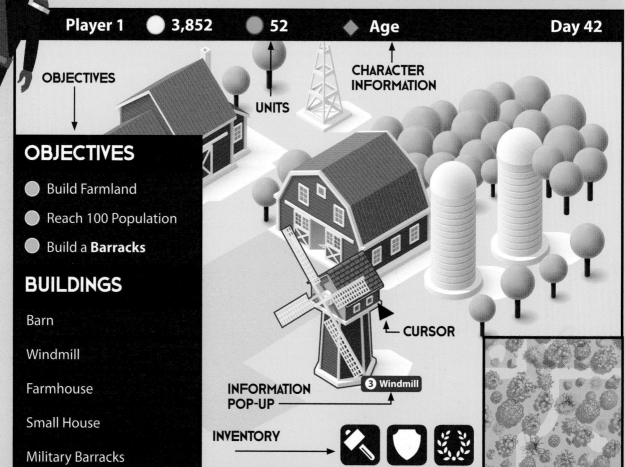

Player 1   3,852   52   Age   Day 42

OBJECTIVES

UNITS

CHARACTER INFORMATION

OBJECTIVES

- Build Farmland
- Reach 100 Population
- Build a **Barracks**

BUILDINGS

Barn

Windmill

Farmhouse

Small House

Military Barracks

CURSOR

INFORMATION POP-UP

3 Windmill

INVENTORY

REAL-TIME STRATEGY

Also called RTS games, these feature action that plays out in real time. Sometimes you can pause the action to give your orders, but the focus is on fast-paced action.

TURN-BASED STRATEGY

Like a lot of the board games that inspire this **genre**, turn-based strategy games let players take turns to make their move, giving you a bit more time to think.

TOWER DEFENSE

This popular game type involves players dropping towers into specific locations to fend off waves of incoming enemies.

MULTIPLAYER ONLINE BATTLE ARENAS

MOBAs for short, these games (such as League of Legends and DOTA 2) have teams of players that control powerful heroes and take down the opposing team's base.

GRAND STRATEGY

Some games can be quick matches that just take a few minutes. Grand strategy games, however, will play out over hours, days, weeks, and maybe longer.

MILITARY HISTORY

A lot of strategy games are inspired by real historical **conflicts**, with whole games based on individual battles as well as longer wars.

MANAGEMENT SIMULATIONS

Whether you want to build a city, run a sports club, or set up a space station, management **simulation** games let you take control of a business or organization.

FACT FILE: SID MEIER'S CIVILIZATION

It could be argued that Sid Meier's **Civilization** is the most important strategy game ever made. The game's objective is to "build an empire to stand the test of time." The game has certainly done that.

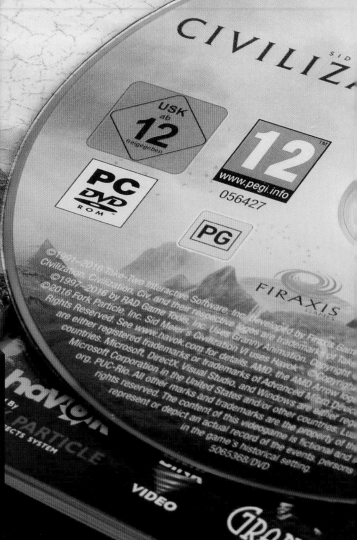

The first Civilization game was launched all the way back in 1991. This series is mostly played on a PC. There are now six main games, but along the way we've had plenty of **spin-offs**, including simplified console and mobile versions, board games, and even a futuristic game called Civilization: Beyond Earth.

Over the years, we've seen a steady stream of new features and improvements being made to the game. From the beginning, the objective has been to take a civilization from the year 4000 B.C.E., grow your lands over the centuries, and become the most powerful empire in the world. You can grow your civilization a number of ways, but the simplest is to hire soldiers to battle your neighbors and take their land. Civilization is a 4X game, which means explore, expand, **exploit**, and **exterminate**. Players must explore their surroundings, expand their empire, exploit their resources, and exterminate anyone who stands in their way.

But you don't have to fight wars in order to win this game. You can also win a **Culture** Victory by creating Great Works, such as statues and artworks, or by attracting the most tourists from other civilizations. Maybe you'd rather win a Science Victory by becoming the first civilization to colonize Mars!

TECH TALK

If you're going to get ahead in strategy games, you need to know what you're talking about. This data file will help you plan your attacks and think ahead. Okay, Arcade, tell us what we need to know.

<<LOADING... DATA LEVEL THREE: WHAT YOU NEED TO KNOW>>

PLAYER INFO

Play alone in **tutorial** mode or the main game. Play against the computer or against other players online. Some games are made for one player, while others allow you to play in a team.

ADD-ONS

Add-ons are things you plug into the console or PC to add features to the game. Most people prefer to play with a mouse and keyboard. Some even buy a special mouse with programmable buttons, or a light-up keyboard.

VISUALS

Most screens will feature a map. Because you look down on most of these games from above, and the map doesn't move that much, the **animations** and **graphics** can be very detailed.

CONTROLS

On a PC, you often use the keys to plan your moves and give commands, such as moving troops or giving villagers a job to do.

LEVELS

Some games have levels, allowing you to track your progress. Others will have a long **campaign** mode, and you measure success by how powerful you become.

WORLD RECORD HOLDERS

In 2014, two friends from Montana broke the world record for the longest video game marathon while playing a strategy game. JJ Locke and Jeff Nation are part of a group of gamers known as the Great Falls Gamers. Locke and Nation played StarCraft II: Heart of the Swarm, which is part of the StarCraft universe owned and created by Blizzard Entertainment. The pair played for 44 hours without stopping, setting a world record that remains unbroken.

Locke and Nation, along with the rest of the Great Falls Gamers, including Casey Coffman, Jeff Sagedal, and George Vogl, hold two world records:
- Longest video game marathon on a role-playing game: 48 hours 14 minutes (The Elder Scrolls V: Skyrim)
- Longest video game marathon playing a real-time strategy game: 44 hours (StarCraft II: Heart of the Swarm)

1. HOW DID YOU GUYS GET INTO GAMING?

Jeff N: I got into gaming when I was about three or four, playing Sega and Windows computer games.

JJ: I got into games in middle school with a neighbor of mine, and we played a game called Diablo 2 for the PC. It was his dad's game!

Casey: I got into gaming at the age of two when my mother would play Doom II with me! I had most of the game memorized and would warn my mother of where the enemies were.

2. WHAT DO YOU THINK MAKES A GOOD VIDEO GAME?

Jeff N: It has to have a great story, feel adventurous, and be **interactive** with the characters or environment.

JJ: Personally, I like a little challenge and a good story with humor in it, or games that make you think to solve quests.

Jeff S: I like a game that is replayable, like Skyrim, and is story-heavy, with great graphics.

Casey: I want a game to make me feel something, whether it's excitement or sadness. I also want the game to play well.

3. WHY DID YOU WANT TO BREAK THE WORLD RECORD?

Jeff N: When I was younger, I was fascinated by world records. So I told myself one day I would be in there somehow, and it turned out to be through gaming!

Jeff S: Not many people break world records in gaming. Gaming is what I love. So my friends and I came together to make magic happen! It was something to say that I did for later in life.

Casey: I honestly just thought it would be fun. It's pretty cool to see my name and picture in the World Record book!

4. WHAT STRATEGIES DID YOU USE TO GET THROUGH SUCH A MARATHON?

Jeff N: We are allowed a little break time while we play, so sometimes I took a break just to get fresh air, and check on the record team too, since I was the one leading this record.

Jeff S: I think the general strategy was to alternate sleep and bathroom breaks. I was the last to get sleep at the 40-hour mark. I slept for 18 straight hours on the drive home and at the house back home!

From left to right, JJ Locke, Jeff Nation, George Vogl, and Casey Coffman.

5. WHAT ADVICE WOULD YOU GIVE CHILDREN WHO WANT TO GET INTO GAMING?

Jeff N: There is a game out there for everybody, whether it's RPG, First Person Shooters, RTS (Real-Time Strategy), or team shooters like Overwatch. Just play!

JJ: Don't start with competitive games like StarCraft II or League of Legends. Those games aren't for beginners! Start with fun, non-competitive ones until you get a good understanding of games and how they work. Then, if you want, try the competitive ones.

Jeff S: If you want to make games, programming would be the way to go. They also have colleges for game development as well.

Casey: Play games that make you happy. I really don't think there is any other better advice than that. Find a game that looks really good to you and play the heck out of it!

PLANNING A STRATEGY

In strategy games, knowledge is power. Understanding all the different elements that make up each decision will put you on the path to VICTORY!

<<LOADING... DATA LEVEL FOUR: ELEMENTS OF STRATEGY>>

UNITS

Units can include soldiers, builders, ships, workers, scouts, aerial units (such as airplanes), and more. Most units can be moved around and given different commands. For example, a unit of soldiers can be told to advance and attack or to patrol an area.

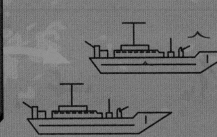

BUILDINGS

Your army or empire is powered by the buildings you can construct. For example, a barracks will allow you to train soldiers, or a factory can be used to build tanks. Building homes allows you to increase your population, and some games include buildings such as libraries, where you can research new technologies.

RESOURCES

Resources, such as food, weapons, or more troops, must be increased. Most games will place resources around the map which you can send units to collect.

ROCK, PAPER, SCISSORS

The key to success is to know which units to use for what job. Just like rock, paper, scissors, certain units are more effective against others. For example, you might find that **cavalry** are strong against **infantry**, but weak against **archers**.

DEFENSE

It's important to build defensive walls, **fortify** your position with weapons and troops, and take advantage of the best locations on the map.

TERRAIN

Terrain can range from rocky mountains or sandy beaches to grassy fields or thick forests. A location with lots of resources will be useful but other people will want to take them. Forests can be great for hiding in to surprise an opponent. Coastlines can be great for fishing and travel. Knowing how to work with your environment is an important part of your strategy.

SPEED & TIME

Some games can be paused so you can plan your next move. Take as much time as you can to look at your surroundings and what your opponents are doing. Once you've made your plan, it's important to make your move as fast as possible so you can surprise your enemy.

CHESS AND GO

Strategy gaming in video games started in traditional board games, such as Chess and Go. As video games became more popular, these games started to move onto PCs and then consoles. As computer programming improved, people started to be able to play against a computer instead of needing another player in the room. With the arrival of the Internet, players could have a game of chess with someone on the other side of the world! There are a lot of similarities between the two, with many strategy video games using the same layout, pieces, and board setup as the original video games they are based on.

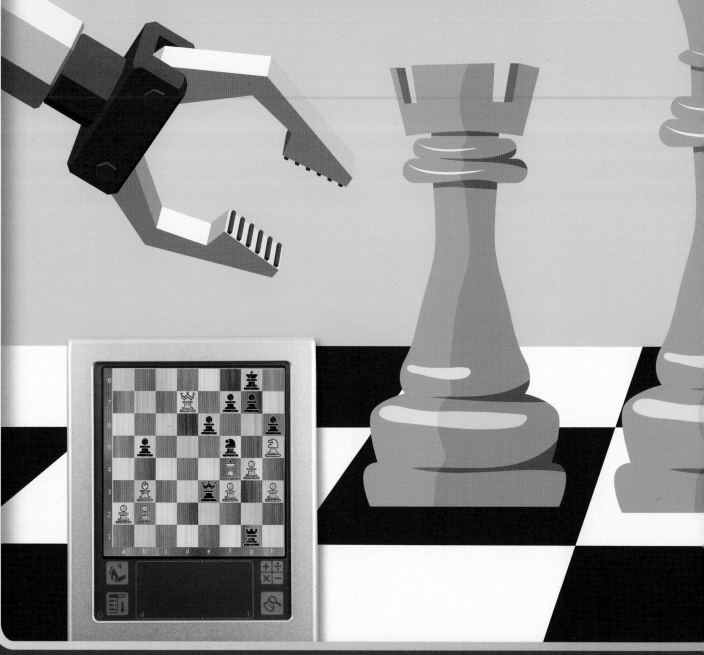

Some of the oldest forms of games we know about are strategy games. Go, a game where you move black or white counters to try and surround your opponent's counters, was invented in China more than 2,500 years ago. It is believed to be the oldest board game still played today. Chess is believed to have been invented in India in the 600s, and it is still played by millions of people around the world. These were some of the first strategy games to move to screens. Early versions were very simple, and many remain so to this day.

The long-lasting popularity of strategy games lies in their unique features. Some players like the competitive element, others enjoy outsmarting their opponents, and some people enjoy the fact that the games can be played for many hours. Others, particularly grand strategy players, like the escape from everyday life. Who wouldn't want to spend their evenings taking over the world, then head safely back into real life the next day?

GET YOUR GAME ON

Okay, so I've decided to be Julius Caesar, leader of the Roman Empire! Before we start, we should make a plan. This is a strategy game, after all. Planning is everything!

<<LOADING... DATA LEVEL FIVE: HOW TO PLAY>>

SETTING IT UP

The first step in any strategy game is getting everything set up the way you want it. You will have lots of choices to make in some of these games. For example, in grand strategy games, you will have to choose which country you want to lead and what to do with your resources. What happens in the game depends on your choices. If you choose to put all your resources into building farms, you might become very rich, but you will have few defenses. If you mostly focus on military moves, you won't get attacked, but you also won't have much to defend! Generally, the more difficult the game, the longer setting it up is likely to take. But some people think this is all part of the fun!

EXPLORATION

Once you have your game set up, the next thing you should do is explore the area around you. This will let you discover what resources you have and who you may need to defend them from! This will also help you to know where your military units will be most useful and how best to get supplies to the troops.

ANTICIPATION

One of the most important things you can do in a strategy game is to **anticipate** what your opponents may do. This will help you to plan your next moves and even lay traps for your opponents. You can also research the newest technologies available so you can stay one step ahead of your competitors.

MIDGAME

In the middle part of the game, you can start to expand and explore further. As you build and develop new technologies, such as sailing and flying, you will be able to discover more of the terrain around you. Build watchtowers, if the game allows, and send out exploring parties. You will start to discover other units and players around you. You may be able to conquer them. This will add to your power and give you one less enemy to worry about. The most important skill here is multitasking, or doing many things at once. But don't forget what your objective in the game is.

<<DID YOU KNOW?>>
SPEED IS KEY. ALWAYS GET YOUR BUILDINGS AND SOLDIERS IN PLACE, YOUR TANKS RUNNING, AND YOUR ARMIES AND RESOURCES BUILT UP AS QUICKLY AS POSSIBLE.

VICTORY...OR FAILURE?

The last stage of the game is called the endgame. Winning the game depends on what objective you had at the beginning of the game. It may be that you win based on how many countries you have conquered. It might even be a race mode, where the first player to meet a certain target, such as developing space travel, is the winner. The endgame is where everything you have planned for has come together. There is no better feeling than knowing that hours of planning, setting up goals, and moving units around has paid off and you are victorious!

8 REASONS VIDEO GAMES ARE GOOD FOR YOU

EYE SPY

Action video games can improve your eyesight. These games help to improve how easily you can tell shades of gray apart. This can give you much better night vision!

DOCTOR, DOCTOR

Hand-eye **coordination** means how well your hands work with your eyes when performing a task. Ever tried to thread a needle? That's hand-eye coordination at work. Scientists think that even surgeons should play video games to improve their hand-eye coordination during surgery!

YOU DECIDE

Games train us to keep track of moving images and to **process** information. This means we are better able to make quick decisions. This is especially true for action games, which involve a lot of running, jumping, climbing, and shooting.

BRAIN BOX

Fast-paced games help develop our ability to easily take in information from many different sources. This helps you to learn and do as well in school as you do in the games!

OLD TIMES

Playing games can slow the aging process, keeping us younger for longer. Just 10 hours a week is enough to slow down aging! Using your mind will help it stay sharp and young.

FOCUS

Playing video games can help your concentration and focus. This can help you pay better attention in school!

JUMP AROUND

Video games can be good for your health! Games such as Wii Sports and **virtual reality** games get you up, out of your seat, and moving!

CAREER LADDER

Many games reward leadership, creative thinking, and providing for others. Scientists think this might mean people who play games regularly get good jobs and are faster to respond in a **crisis**.

FACT FILE: STARCRAFT II

One of the most popular strategy games in the world is StarCraft, made by Blizzard Entertainment. It's a real-time strategy game, or RTS, which means there is no pausing the game. Instead, it's a race to build a strong base to defend against enemy attacks while also building units to take out your opponent.

In the game, there are three groups fighting to control an area in space—the Terrans, the Zerg, and the Protoss. Each group has its own strengths and weaknesses. StarCraft is so popular that some terms from the game are now used by gamers while playing other games. One of these terms is Zerg rush. This refers to the Zerg group and their ability to attack early. StarCraft gamers figured out that by making lots of low-cost units very quickly, they could send a large number of them to their opponent's base in a surprise attack. Now, in any game, whenever one side makes an early attack on an enemy base, the move is often called a Zerg rush.

What makes the StarCraft series stand out is the number of different ways there are to play the game. Players can use different strategies each time they play. This variety makes the game very interesting for players to explore. As well, Blizzard's incredible art design means that exploring the game's possibilities is a visually satisfying experience.

PRO TALK

Let's find out more about games by talking to a professional. Gaming professionals are people who do something in gaming to earn a living, such as make video games or write about them in magazines. These pros really know their stuff. Let's hear some advice and tips from one now.

DAN GRILIOPOULOS

He is currently Lead Writer for the massive simulations and games tech firm Improbable. He was a games journalist for 15 years, he's written for several games, and he's the coauthor of a book about how video games can teach you **philosophy**.

1. WHAT MAKES GAMES FUN TO PLAY WITH YOUR FRIENDS?

"It's the fact that you're playing them with your friends, with their unpredictable, familiar, real behavior! Even the simplest... game—Smash Bros. or Gang Beasts, say—is made so much better by that social relationship."

TEN things VIDEO GAMES CAN teach us
(About Life, Philosophy and Everything)
JORDAN ERICA WEBBER AND DANIEL GRILIOPOULOS

2. WHY DO WE LIKE CHALLENGING AND DIFFICULT GAMES?

"Why do we like challenge in life at all? Because when we strive for something in real life, it is for reward. Games have that too, but failure (mostly) has few **consequences**, and the rewards can be huge. Challenge makes the power and the reward all the sweeter."

3. WHAT MAKES A GREAT VIDEO GAME CHARACTER?

"It depends what the game's creators are trying to show! Mario is **iconic**, with cartoonish animations and catchphrases. But a narrative game—like Horizon: Zero Dawn—will want to establish emotional links with the player's character and show how they change through the story. "

4. WHAT CAN GAMES DO THAT OTHER MEDIUMS CAN'T?

"Interactivity! Other media [such as a movie or a book] are **linear** experiences, but in games you get a choice over your character's actions, personality, and world. Of course, philosophers might say it only feels as if you are in control. A game designer has created every step in the game you're playing, after all."

5. HOW CAN GAMES HELP US BE MORE CREATIVE?

"The best games are **portals** into other worlds. They help show us what other worlds might be like and expand our view of what our own lives could be like."

FACT FILE: WORMS W.M.D™

Worms is an all-time classic that has been entertaining players for many, many years. It's the game that put developer Team17 on the map. Thanks to a blend of cute worms and wickedly sneaky gameplay, the series has stood the test of time.

The setup is refreshingly simple. Players take control of a team of up to eight warriors who just happen to be worms. These slimy little critters might look defenseless, but appearances can be deceiving. These squidgy little soldiers come with a surprising number of weapons!

Ranging from guns and grenades to more interesting options such as exploding sheep, bouncing banana bombs, and giant concrete donkeys, the player has a whole host of options open to them. These weapons are used to take out worms on the opposing team. Players use advantages to line up perfect shots or knock enemies off the map and into the water below.

No two games are the same in Worms. In the most recent entry in the series, Worms W.M.D, there are even buildings that your worms can enter and vehicles for them to drive. As your worms slither across the environment, they can use ninja ropes and jet packs to get around. Players have plenty of opportunities to sneak up on their opponents and hand out sneaky and hilariously explosive attacks.

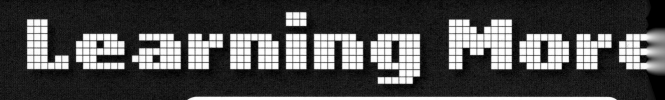

YES! We RULE! Literally! We came, we read, we conquered. We can leave the Arcade now, knowing that our kingdoms are safe and we rule the world! Or, if you're not finished learning, you can go to these websites to find out more...

<<CONTINUE? Y/N>>
HTTPS://CIVILIZATION.COM/

<<CONTINUE? Y/N>>
WWW.GUINNESSWORLDRECORDS.COM/
SEARCH?TERM=VIDEOGAMES

<<CONTINUE? Y/N>>
HTTPS://THEBALANCECAREERS.COM/
VIDEO-GAME-JOBS-525965

<<CONTINUE? Y/N>>
HTTPS://STARCRAFT.COM/EN-US/

<<CONTINUE? Y/N>>
WWW.TEAM17.COM/
GAMES/WORMS-WMD/

<<CONTINUE? Y/N>>
HTTPS://SCRATCH.MIT.EDU/

Glossary

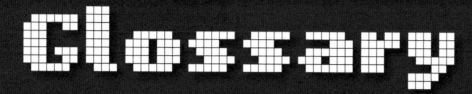

animation	Moving images, such as cartoons
anticipate	To think about and prepare for something in advance
archer	A person who shoots a bow and arrow
barracks	A building or group of buildings where soldiers live
campaign	A continuing storyline or set of adventures
cavalry	The part of an army that serves on horseback
civilization	The society and way of life of a particular area
conflicts	Fights or battles
consequences	The result or effect of an action
console	A computer system that connects video games to a screen
coordination	The ability for people or things to work together properly
crisis	A difficult situation that must be dealt with
culture	The arts and other examples of human achievement
electronic	Describes a device or machine powered by electricity
exploit	To use and benefit from
exterminate	To destroy completely
fortify	To strengthen in preparation against an attack
genre	A particular type of something
graphics	Images and design on a computer screen
iconic	Recognized and admired around the world
infantry	The part of an army that fights on foot
interactive	Flow of information between computer and user
linear	To progress from one stage to another in proper order
objective	The main goal or target
philosophy	The study of ideas about human life, such as right and wrong
portal	A window or doorway to another level or world
process	To take in information and respond to it
resources	Useful supplies of money, materials, or people
simulation	An imitation of a real-world situation
spin-off	A game based on characters or places from other games
strategy	A plan, or series of actions, that will achieve a desired outcome
terrain	The surface features of an area of land
tutorial	A teaching level in which gamers learn the controls for a particular game
virtual reality	A three-dimensional visual world created by a computer that people can interact with while wearing a headset

<<SAVING KNOWLEDGE. DO NOT SHUT DOWN.>>

Index

<<THANKS FOR ACCESSING THE ARCADE TODAY. WE HOPE YOU HAD THE BEST TIME. SHUTTING DOWN IN 3... 2... 1...>>